William Bolcom

Complete Gospel Preludes

for organ

ISBN-13: 978-1-4234-1274-8
ISBN-10: 1-4234-1274-5

EDWARD B. Marks Music Company

Exclusively Distributed By
HAL•LEONARD CORPORATION
7777 W. BLUEMOUND RD. P.O. BOX 13819 MILWAUKEE, WI 53213

www.ebmarks.com
www.halleonard.com

EDITOR'S NOTE

This is the second edition of Books 1, 3, and 4 and the third edition of Book 2. This complete edition was edited by Michael Mazzatenta. An effort has been made to pare down the registration indications from earlier editions and to correct notational errors under the supervision of the composer.

COMMISSIONING INFORMATION

BOOK 1 (1979)
Commissioned by the Dallas, Texas Chapter of the American Guild of Organists on the occasion of the 60th Anniversary of its founding and the dedication of the new organ of the University Park United Methodist Church. First performance April 2, 1979.

BOOK 2 (1980-81)
Commissioned by The Marilyn Mason Commissioning Fund

BOOK 3 (1981)
Commissioned by Walter Holtkamp, Jr. on the occasion of the dedication of the organ in the Chapel at Emory University

BOOK 4 (1984)
Commissioned by The Marilyn Mason Commissioning Fund, made possible by a generous grant from Lorraine Ray

Program notes by Michael Mazzatenta appear on page 88.

CONTENTS

BOOK 1

1. What a Friend We Have in Jesus! 5

2. La Cathédrale engloutie (Rock of Ages) 14

3. Just As I Am 19

BOOK 2

4. Jesus Loves Me 25

5. Shall We Gather at the River (Fantasia) 32

6. Amazing Grace 41

BOOK 3

7. Jesus Calls Us; O'er the Tumult 55

8. Blessed Assurance 58

9. Nearer, My God, to Thee 64

BOOK 4

10. Sometimes I Feel 68

11. Sweet Hour of Prayer 73

12. Free Fantasia on "O Zion, Haste" and "How Firm a Foundation" 76

Extra, not a "Gospel" Prelude

Chorale Prelude on "Abide with Me" (1970) 86

WILLIAM BOLCOM

William Bolcom was born in Seattle, Washington on May 26, 1938 and now resides in Ann Arbor, Michigan, where he is the Ross Lee Finney Distinguished Professor of Composition at the University of Michigan.

At age 11 he entered the University of Washington to study composition privately with John Verrall. Later he studied extensively with Darius Milhaud, both in California and Paris. He received a Master's Degree from Mills College and was the first conferee of a Doctor of Music Degree from Stanford University. Among his other honors are the 1988 Pulitzer Prize in Music for his *12 New Etudes for Piano*, two Guggenheim fellowships, two Koussevitzky Foundation grants and an award from the American Academy of Arts and Letters. Additional awards include the Marc Blitzstein Award for Musical Theater, two Grammy awards for his recorded settings of William Blake's *Songs of Innocence and of Experience*, and the Henry Russel Award (the University of Michigan's highest academic prize) and Lectureship, and his 1992 investiture in the American Academy of Arts and Letters.

Bolcom has been commissioned by the New York Philharmonic, the Philadelphia Orchestra, the Saint Louis Symphony, the Vienna Philharmonic, the Baltimore Symphony, the National Symphony, the Seattle Symphony, the St. Paul Chamber Orchestra, the Boston Symphony Orchestra (including a new major new choral and orchestral work for 2008), The Boston "Pops" Orchestra, the Chamber Music Society of Lincoln Center, the Pacific Symphony, the American Composers Orchestra, the Metropolitan Opera Orchestra and the Orpheus Ensemble, among others. Chamber commissions and premieres have come from Carnegie Hall Centennial, Yo-Yo Ma and Emanuel Ax, Benita Valente, the Aspen Music Festival, Beaux Arts Trio, Isaac Stern and the Emerson Quartet, the United Nations Charter, the Van Cliburn Piano Competition, the American Guild of Organists, and the Philadelphia Chamber Music Society among many others.

Bolcom has composed three operas, all commissioned by the Lyric Opera of Chicago: *A Wedding* (2004), *A View From the Bridge* (1999), and *McTeague* (1992). He has also composed three theater operas: *Casino Paradise* (1990), *Dynamite Tonite* (1963), and *Theatre of the Absurd* (1970). His stage works have also been presented at the Metropolitan Opera, Portland Opera, Indiana University, Prince Theater (Philadelphia), Opera Theater of Pittsburgh, and Opera Hagen (Germany). Bolcom's operas and other stage works, numerous song cycles, and four books of *Cabaret Songs* were written to texts by longtime collaborator Arnold Weinstein.

As a solo pianist and concert artist with his wife, mezzo-soprano Joan Morris, Bolcom has recorded and performed widely. His music, from ragtime to theater and from chamber to symphonic works, has gained worldwide prominence, and may be heard on the Albany, Argo, CRI, Nonesuch, New World, BMG/RCA, Deutsche Grammophone, Laurel, Crystal, Koch, Newport, Vox, Centaur, Naxos and many other labels. William Bolcom's publisher is Edward B. Marks Music Company (**www.ebmarks.com**).

1. What a Friend We Have in Jesus!

WILLIAM BOLCOM

Jubilant! ♩. = 46; strict time, rhythmic

NB. Accidentals apply throughout beamed groups.
Thus: [notation] ; but: [notation] are both A♭.

Copyright © 1980 by EDWARD B. MARKS MUSIC COMPANY, New York, N.Y. 10016
International Copyright Secured   All Rights Reserved   Printed in U.S.A.

f
mf
f
ff
ff
Gt.
ff
sffz
sffz
sffz
sffz
f
Sw.
cresc.
ff
fist
gliss.
f
mf
f

7

8

mp
p
p
p
cresc. molto
Gt.
cresc. molto
Triumphant!
Gt.
ff
Sw.
f
ff
Gt.
Sw.

10

Quiet the tune sustained

12

Jan. 19, 1979 Minneapolis

2. La Cathédrale engloutie
(Rock of Ages)

Manuals

Pedal

Slowly growing, not rushed

' = normal pause; ϟ = very short; 𝄐 = long; 𝄐 = very long.

Copyright © 1980 by EDWARD B. MARKS MUSIC COMPANY, New York, N.Y. 10016
International Copyright Secured   All Rights Reserved   Printed in U.S.A.

15

Move ahead slightly

(clusters)

cresc. poco a poco to ⊗

(both black & white keys)

add stops slowly

accel. poco a poco
Maestoso 𝅝 = c. 30
(ff)
ff
fff
Full organ
R.H. smooth as possible
sempre fff

Sw.
ff
ff
dim. poco a poco
reduce stops, as possible
3
p
non rit.!
ancora dim.
pp
pp
As at beginning
as at beginning
pp
stops as at beginning
pp
smooth as possible

Jan. 21, 1979 Minneapolis

3. Just As I Am

20

*Trade hands only if necessary.

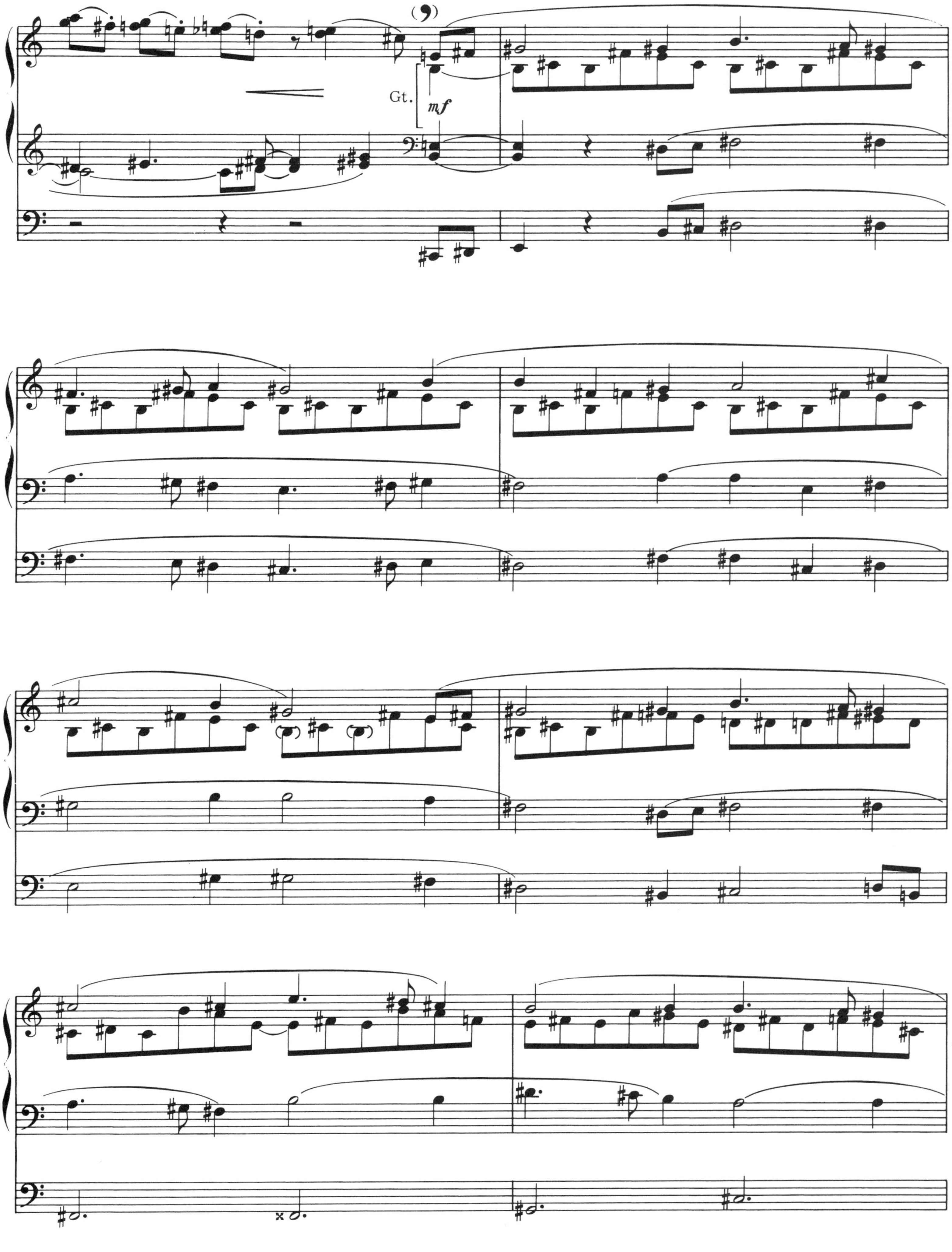
Gt.
mf

22

Broad
espr.
ff not harsh
Sw.
ff to balance on Gt.
ff
ff
to balance others

Feb. 8, 1979 Ann Arbor

4. Jesus Loves Me

WILLIAM BOLCOM

Moderato, tranquil but steady and rhythmically swinging ♪. = c. 60

10
13
Solo 8, or Pos.
Cantabile, semplice
p
pp
+16' pp
16
sempre
simile
18

20
22
poco cresc.
Sw.
p
molto legato, the outer parts and pedal
poco
25
poco
dim.
Pos. or Gt.
different color
sempre legato
pp
Sw.
pp
28
cresc.

28

39
cresc.
smooth
41
With joyful energy
Gt.
43
f
simile
4' 8' 16'
f
45
ff
f

47
ff
f
(f)
49
Pos.
p
dim. molto
A tempo, more and more tranquil
poco tratt
51
Solo or Pos. 4' 8' 16'
*
Sw. 8' 16'
pp
p
simile
53
sim.
*

Sept. 11, 1980 Ann Arbor

5. Shall We Gather at the River
(Fantasia)

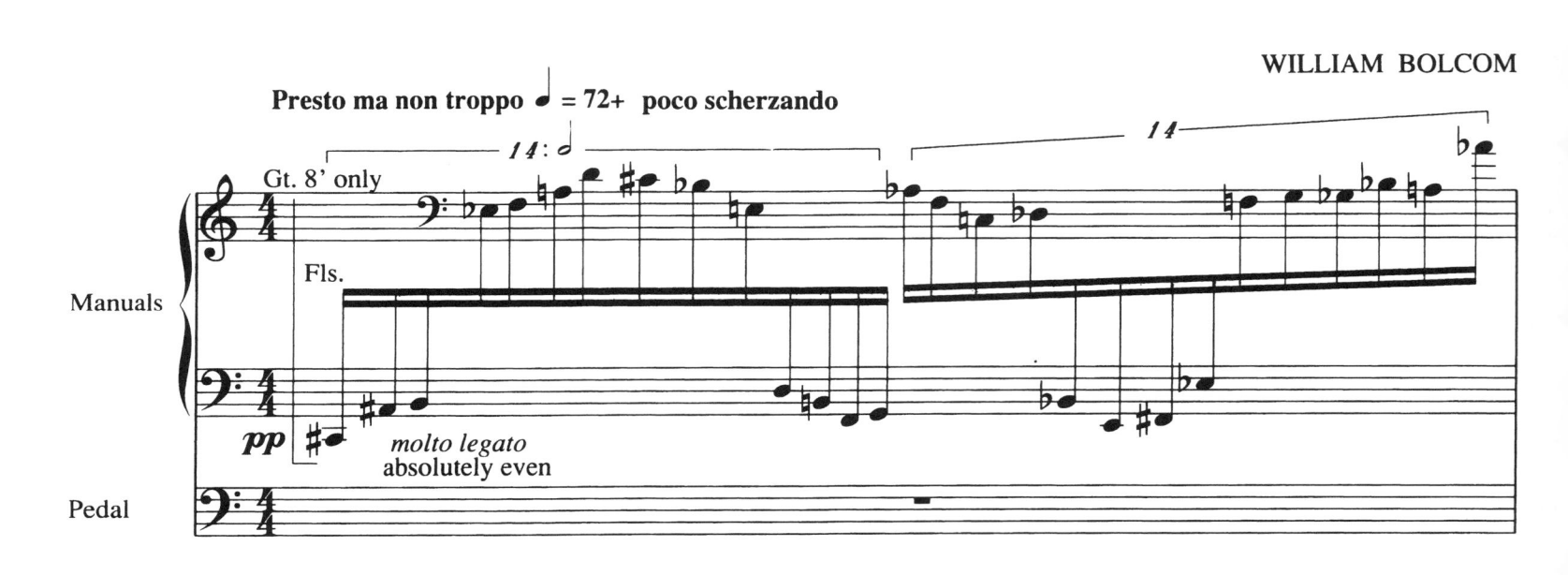

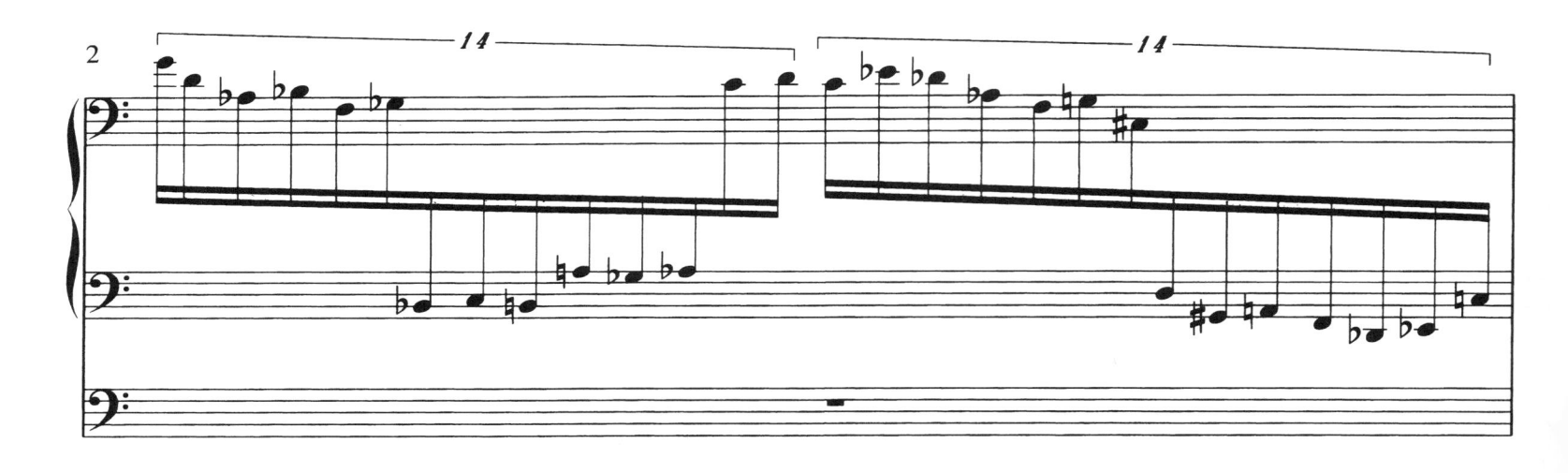

WILLIAM BOLCOM

33

12
Brilliant sound
Full organ
15
fff
smooth
pp
Sw.
8' only
17
8' only
Gt. or Pos. p
(pp)
20

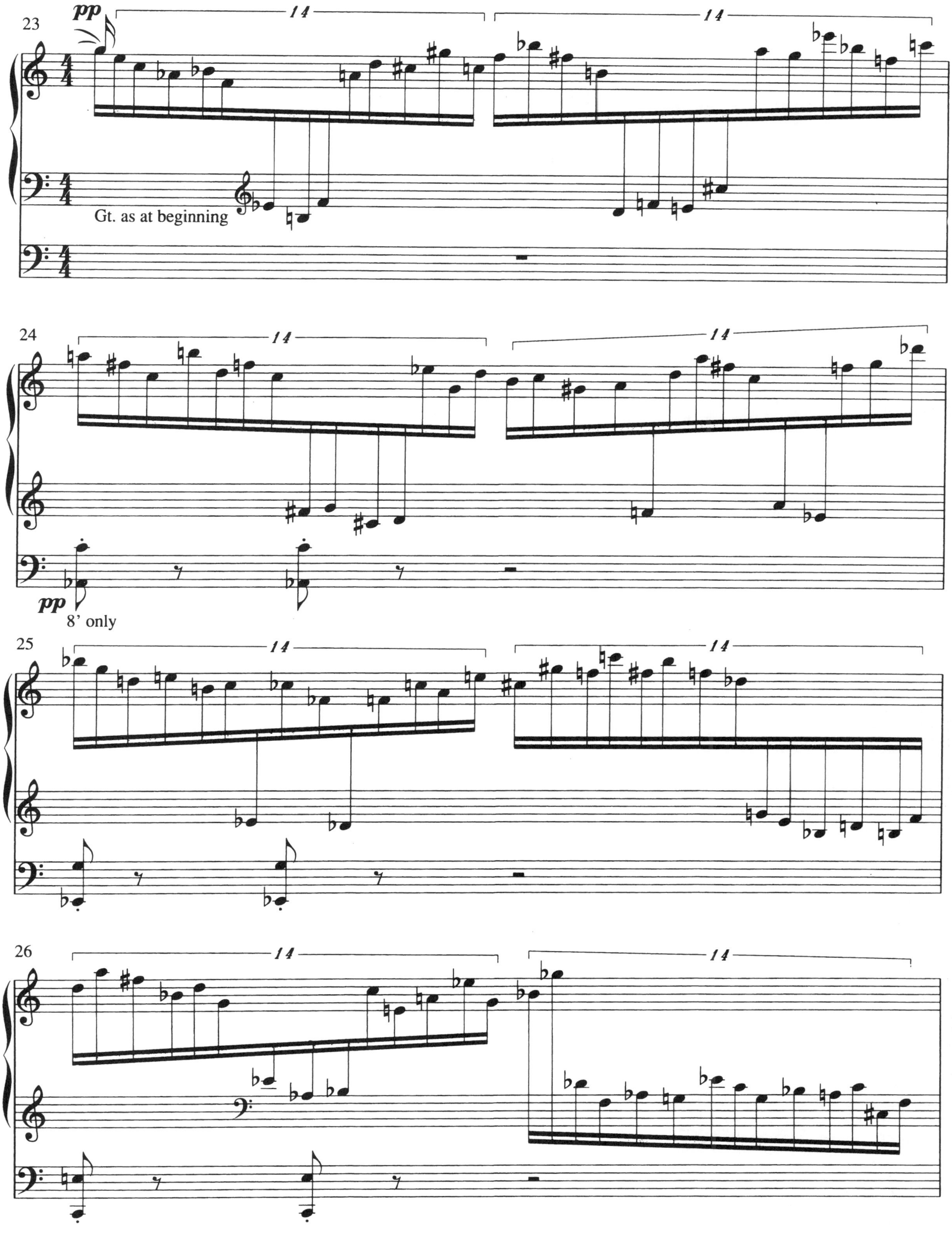
23
pp
14
14
Gt. as at beginning
24
pp
8' only
25
26

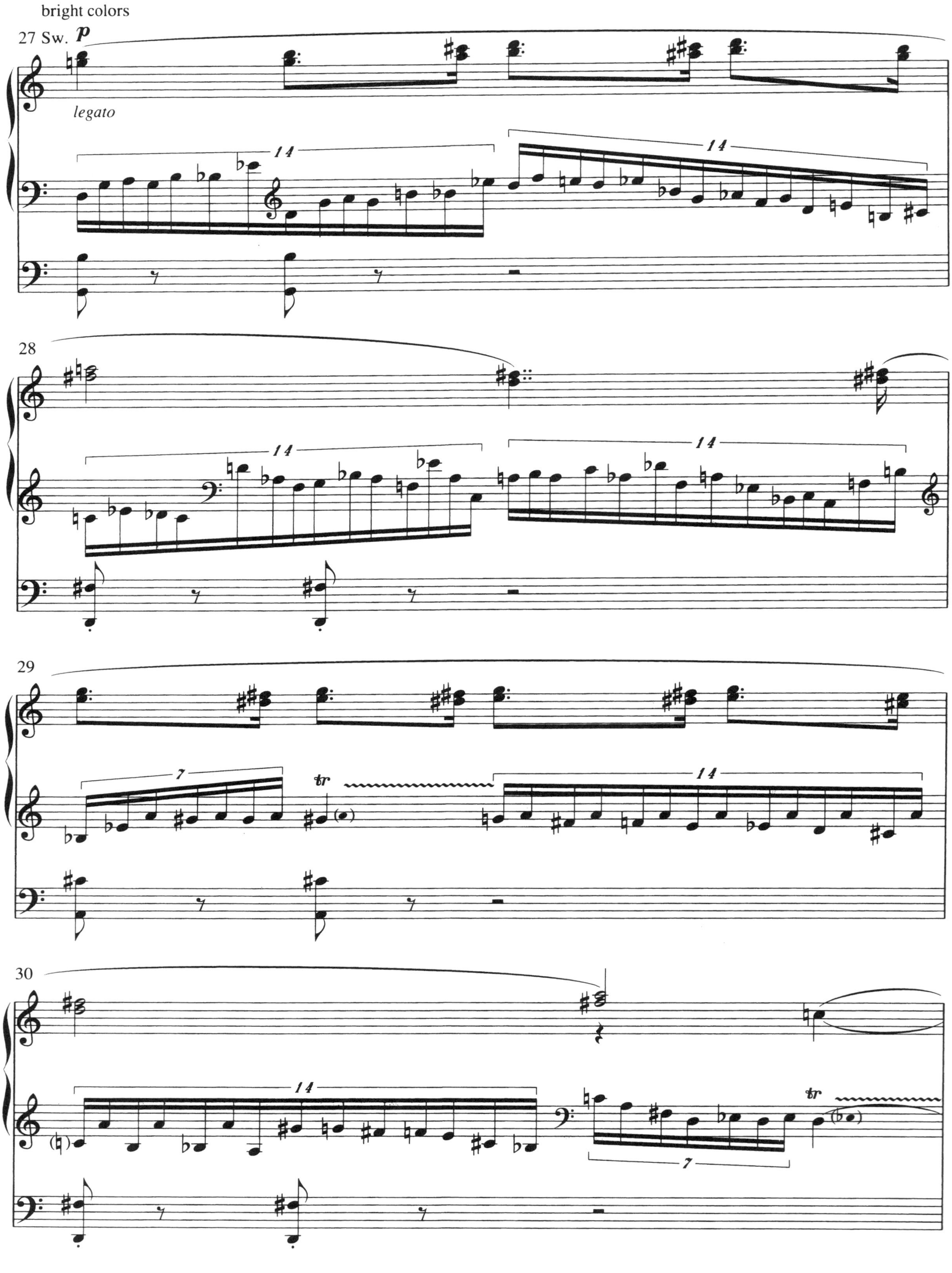
bright colors
27 Sw. p
legato
14
14
28
14
14
29
7
tr
14
30
14
7
tr

[Octaves may be played in the Pedal to m. 50]

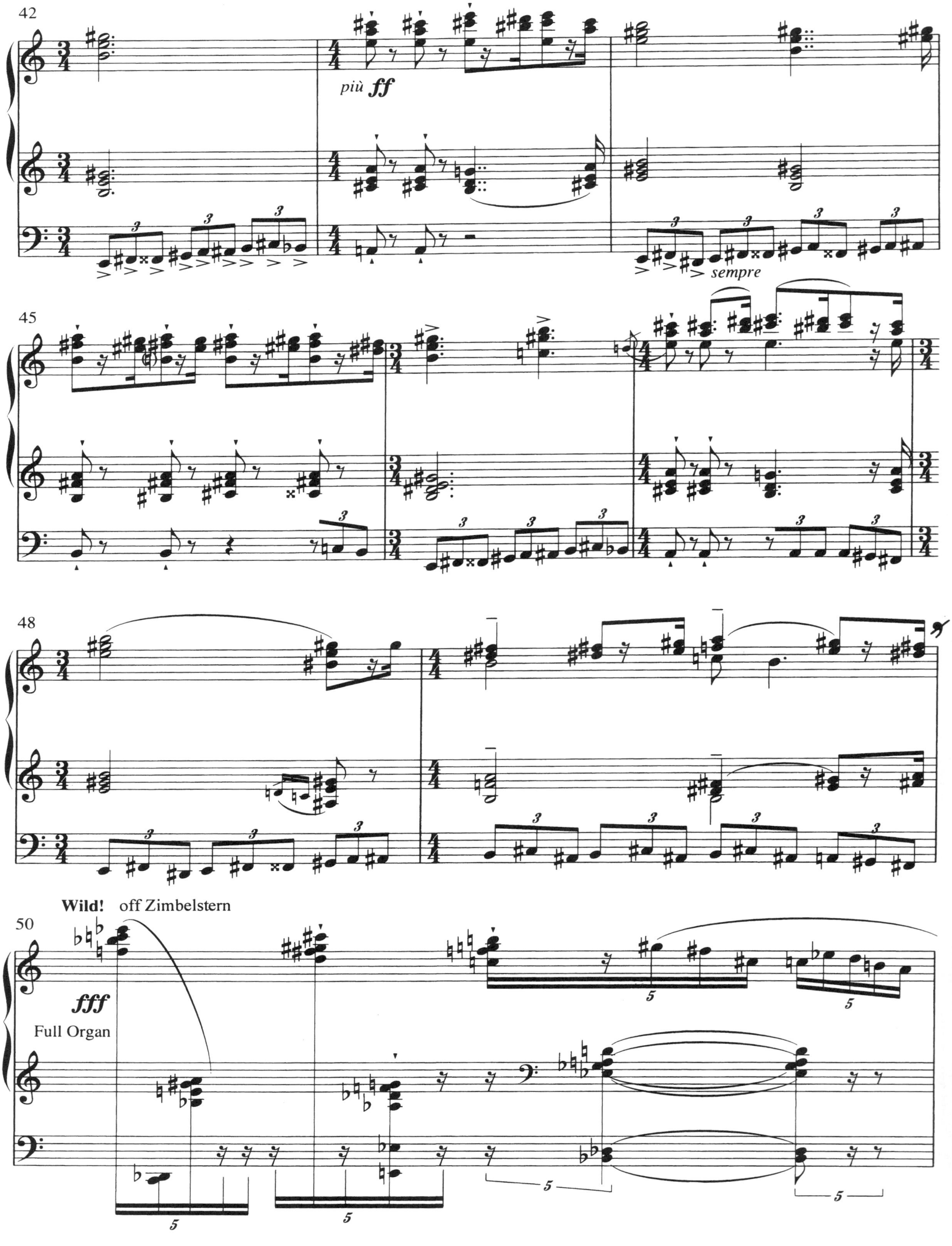
42
più ff
sempre
45
48
Wild!
off Zimbelstern
50
fff
Full Organ

51
12
14
fz
rit.
slow
down
trill
tr
dim.
pp
Sw:reduce to 8'
53
Slower, peaceful
Pos. 8' only
p smooth
move smoothly from
manual to manual
14
pp
Gt. 8' only
(pp) Sw.
pp 8' 16'
56
poco accel.
to →
Tempo I
molto legato
7
Gt.
58

Apr. 30, 1981 Ann Arbor

6. Amazing Grace

WILLIAM BOLCOM

* This R.H. chord is not absolutely important as such. End the glissando neatly.

14
mf
f
16
(𝄿)
mf
ffz
ff
gliss.
ff
ff
ff
18
reduce with diminuendo
fp
mp
fp
dim.
p
p
Variation 1
new color
20
sempre stacc.
(simile)

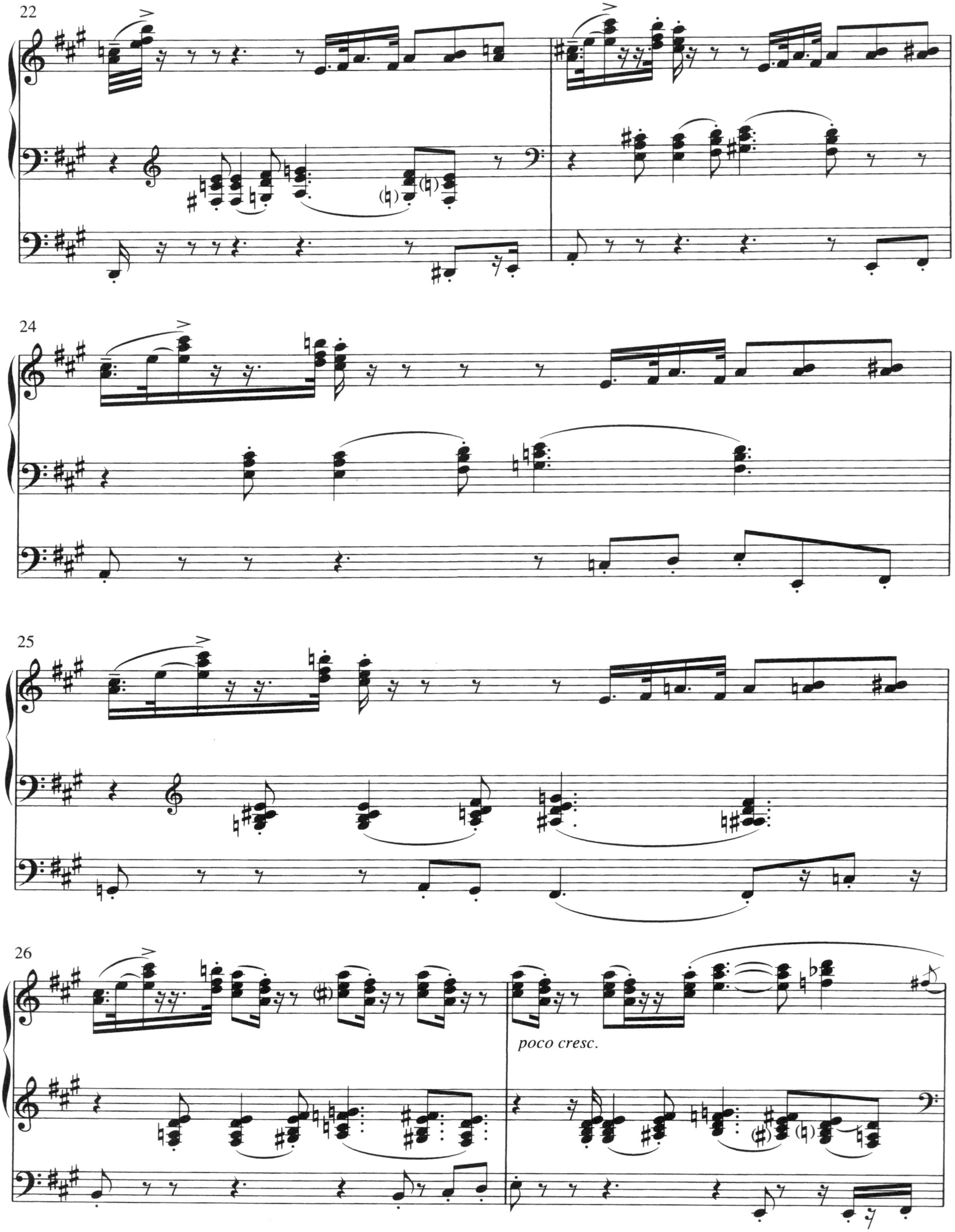
22
24
25
26
poco cresc.

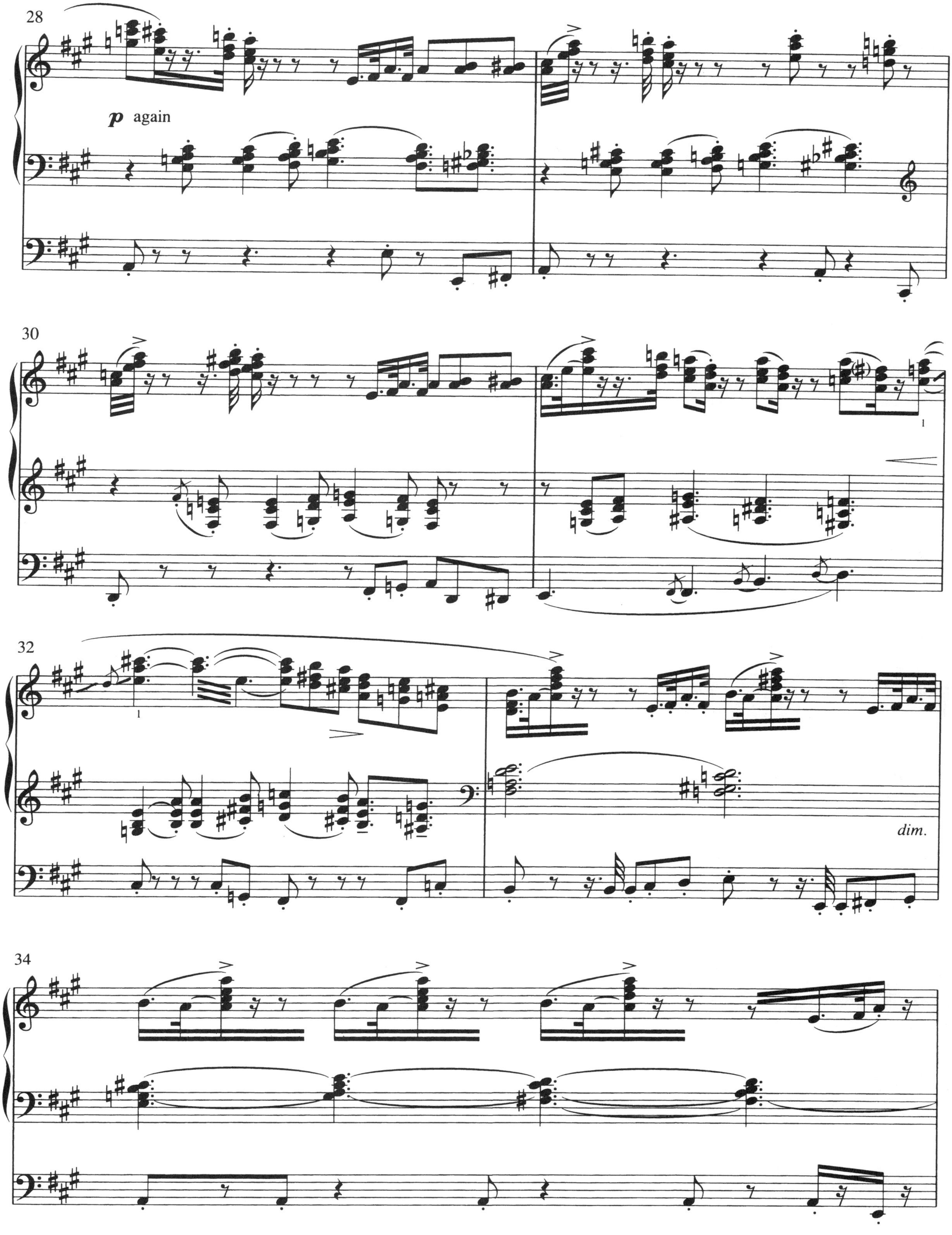
28
p again
30
32
dim.
34

Variation 2
Same Tempo
new color

(smooth, mostly legato throughout, but also very rhythmic and graceful)

add 4' *mp+*, not too prominent

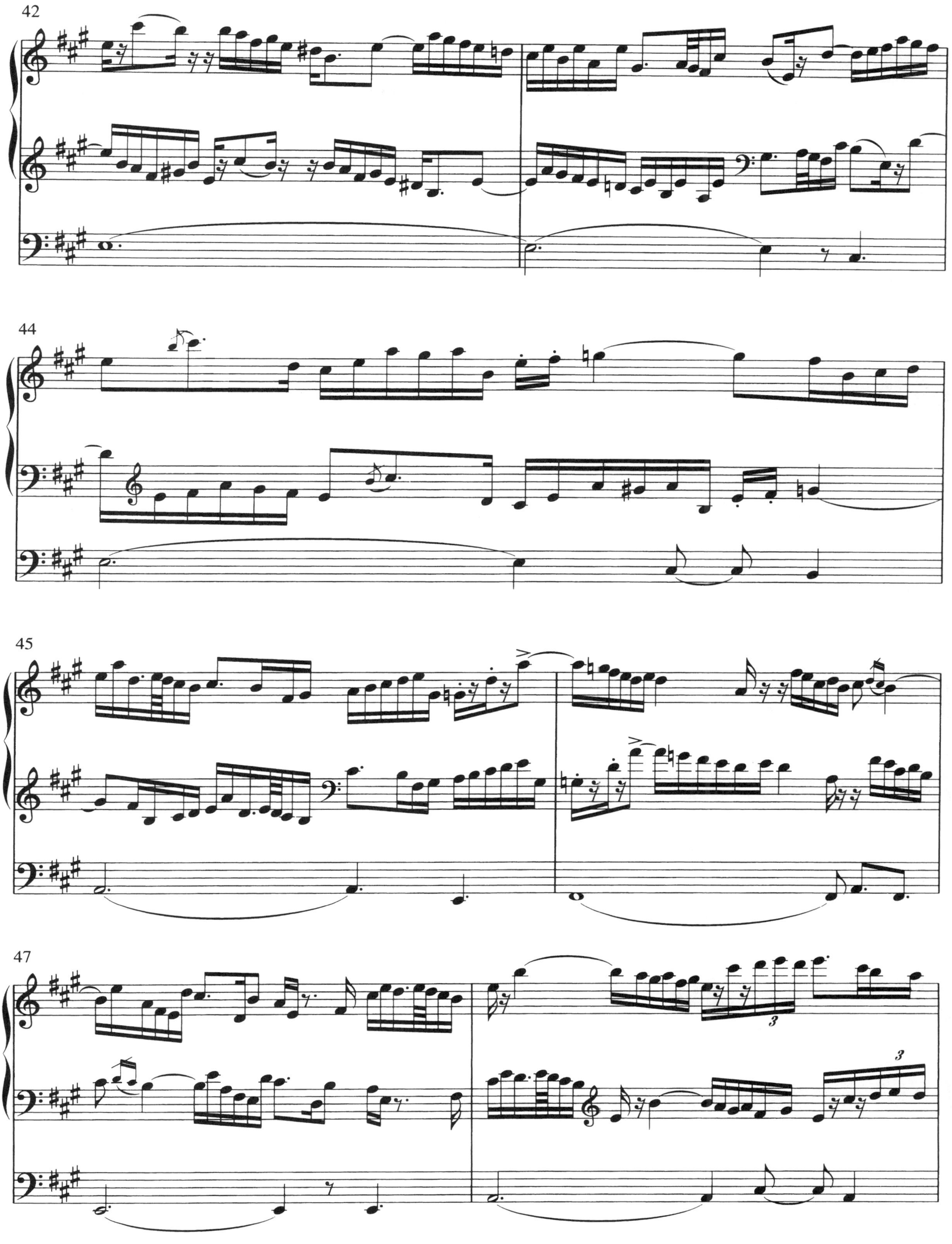
42
44
45
47

49
51
all 8' only
Variation 3
rests are always
exactly counted
Gt.
pp
Sw. ppp
Gt. pp
pp peaceful, simple stops
ppp
pp
16' only, to go well with both Gt. & Sw.
53
Sw.
ppp
Gt.
pp
Sw. ppp
Gt. pp
ppp
pp
ppp
pp
55
Sw.
ppp
Gt.
pp
Sw. ppp
Gt.
pp
ppp
pp
ppp
pp

57
(non cresc.)
Sw. ppp
Gt. pp
Sw. ppp
ppp
pp
59
p Gt.
Sw. pp
mp
Gt.
p
pp
mp
pp
61
cresc.poco a poco
Sw.
pp
Gt.
pp
Sw.
Gt.
63
Sw.
Gt.
Sw.
Gt.

50

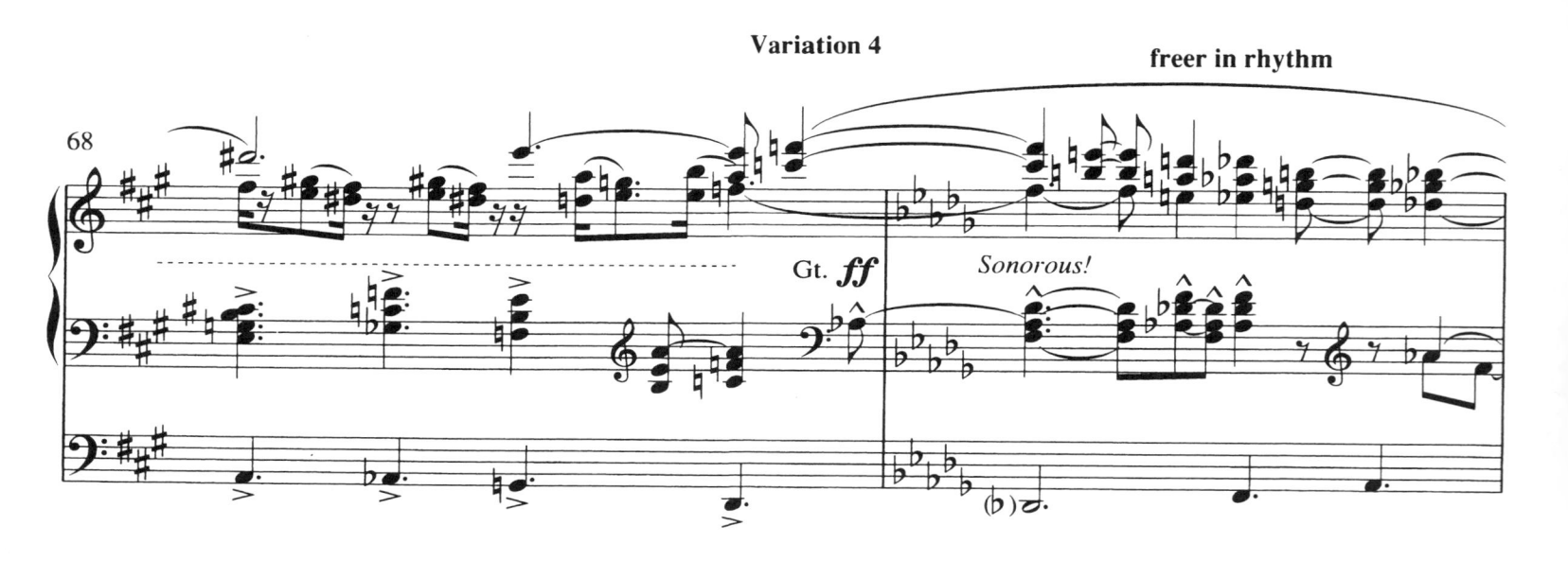

51

78
Sw.
Gt.
ff
poco rit. to
80
dim.
pp
fff
reduce stops to first registration
close Cresc. Ped. slowly
Variation 5: Finale
Tempo I, strict again
82
p
l.h. very smooth (but replay repeated notes)
molto staccato to end
Sempre stacc.
84
p
espr.
mf

87
Pos.:(or r.h. legato) solo,
8' only, cantabile, very simple
mp
89
simile
92
95

May 16, 1981 Ann Arbor

7. Jesus Calls Us; O'er the Tumult

Swell: Krumhorn or other reed 8'
Great: Flute 8'
Pedal: Flute 16' and 8'

WILLIAM BOLCOM
1981

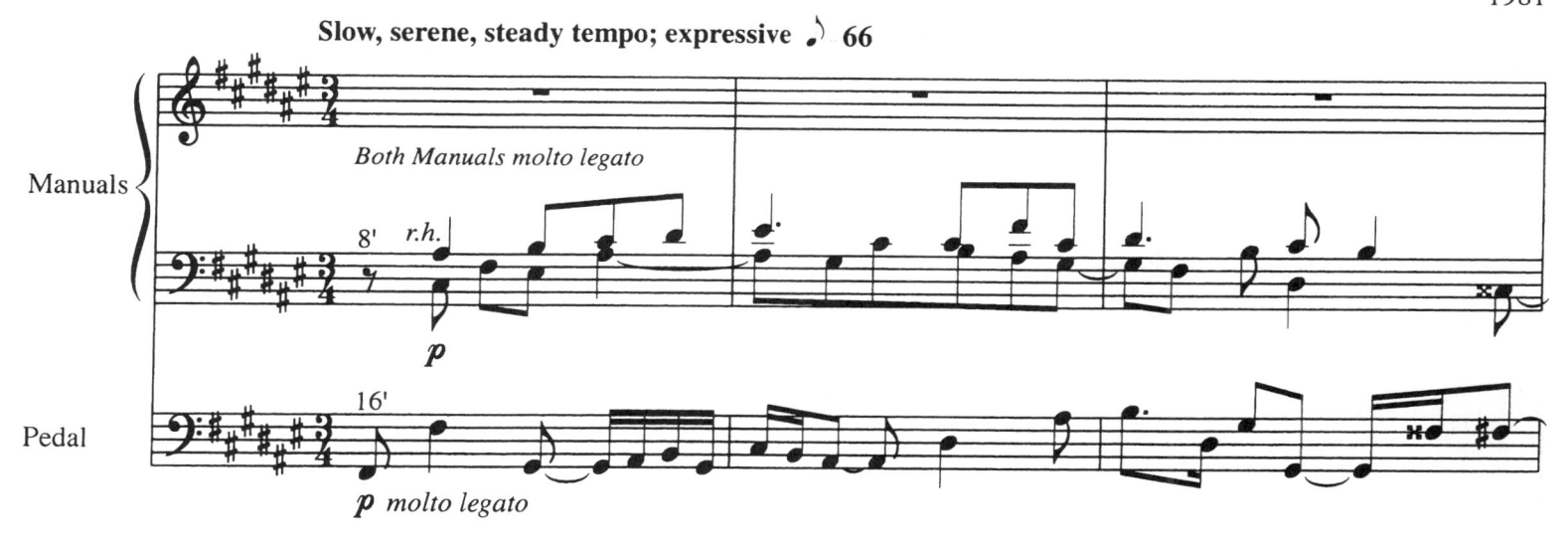

NB: Gospel Preludes 7 through 9 are designed to be played without interruption, but may be performed singly.

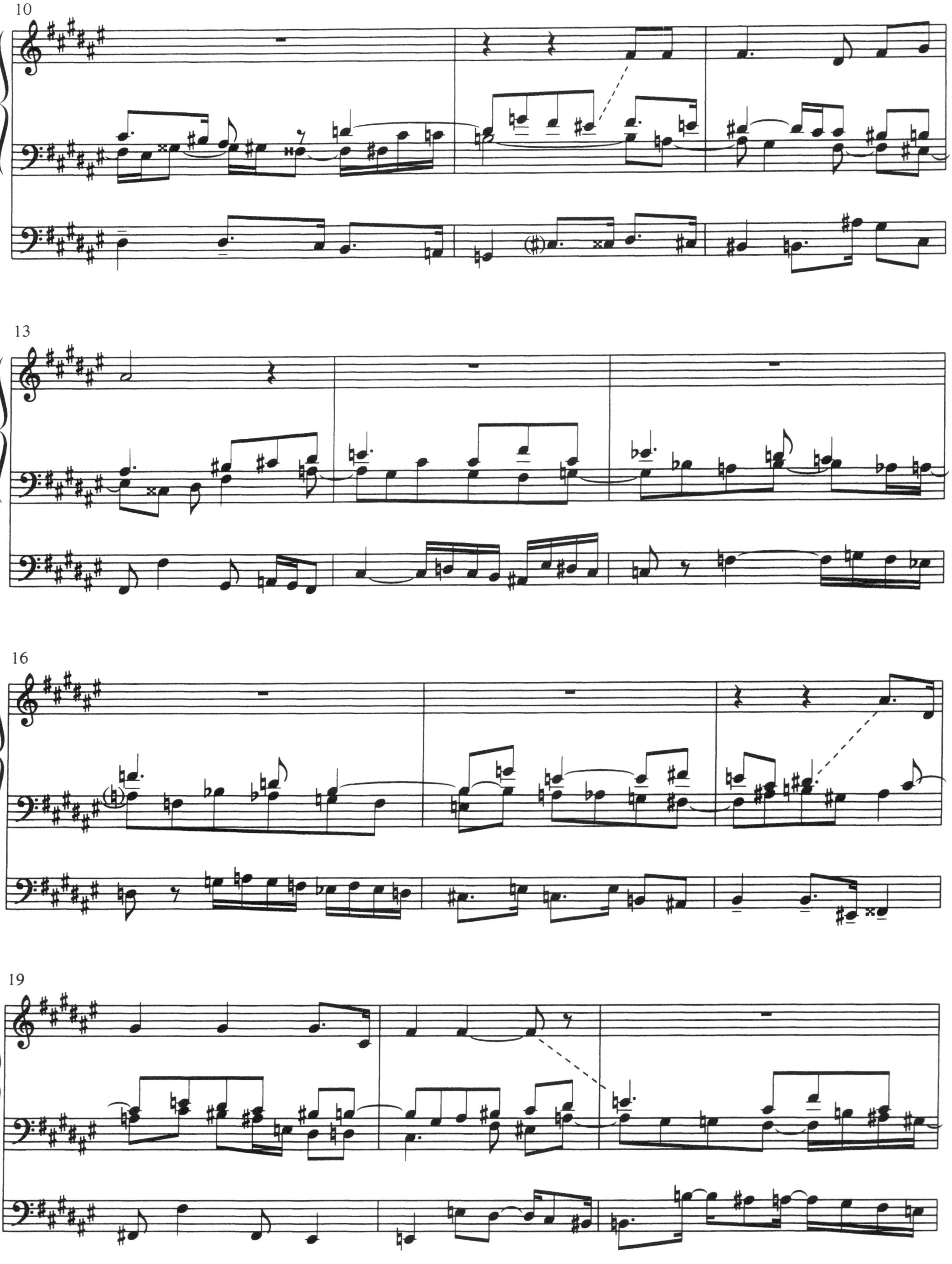
10
13
16
19

Sept. 1, 1981 Ann Arbor

8. Blessed Assurance

Swell: Flute 8', Principal 4', IV, light Trompette or Oboe 8'
Great: Principal 8' 4' 2' foundations
    Swell/Great
Pedal: Bourdon 16', Principal 8'
    Great/Pedal

WILLIAM BOLCOM

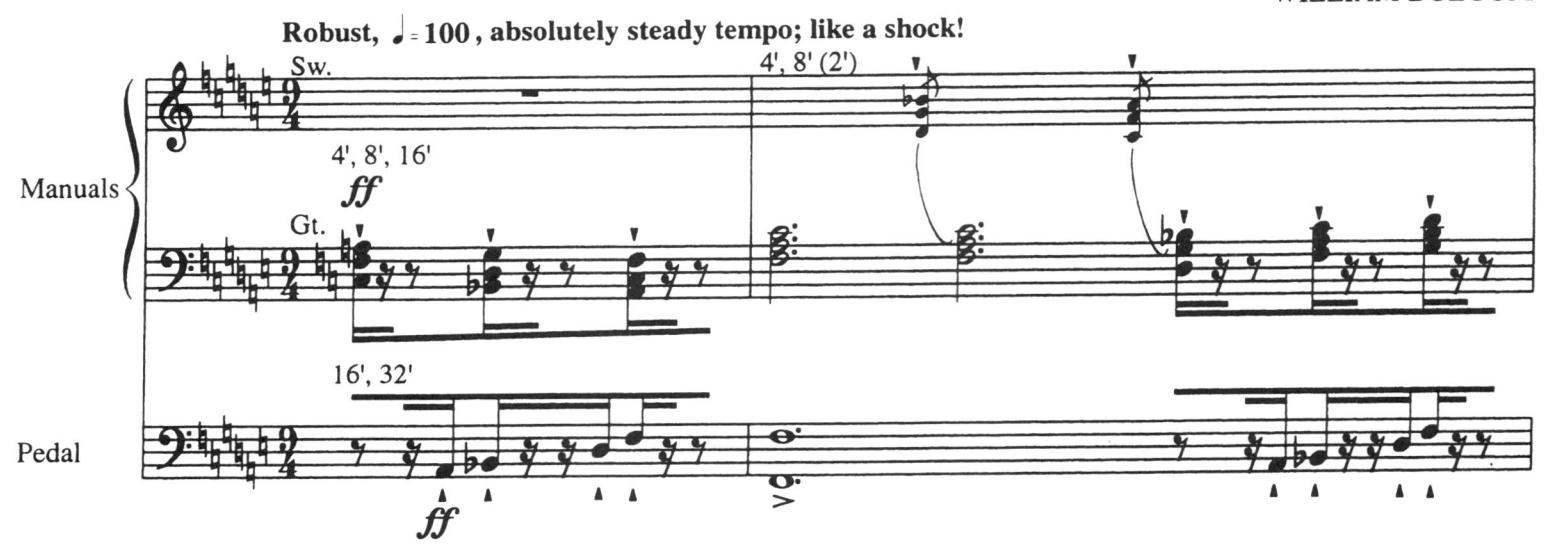

Robust, ♩= 100 , **absolutely steady tempo; like a shock!**

7
9
switch manuals
Swell add 16'
fff
fff
10
12
8
add 16' (if not on already)
fff

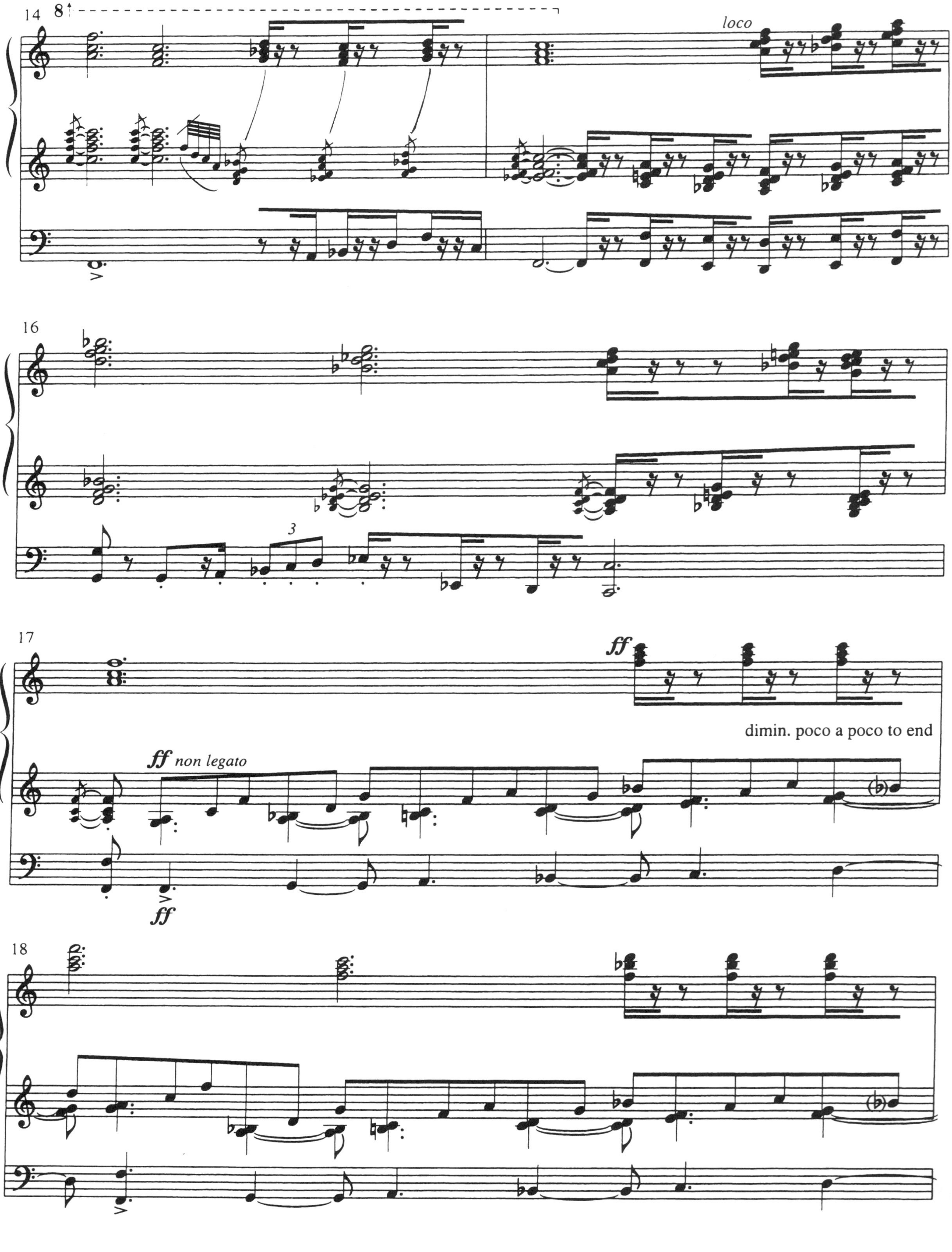
14
8
loco
16
3
17
ff
dimin. poco a poco to end
ff non legato
ff
18

61

23
ancora dim.
24
(still strong)
25
Gt. Prin. 2' off
Sw. IV off
less aggressive
mf
26

Sept. 5, 1981 Ann Arbor

attacca

9. Nearer, My God, to Thee

WILLIAM BOLCOM

*If played separately, start with 'tied-over' chords *ppp*, wait a few seconds before introducing the l.h. A♭, then go on as normal.

Copyright © 1984, 1994 by Edward B. Marks Music Company and Bolcom Music.
International Copyright Secured   All Rights Reserved

*At the Emory University premiere, 6 handbells were used by another player: and this seems **the best solution,** although organ chimes are acceptable.

accelerando poco a poco
Sw. add reeds 16', 8'
Gt.
Sw.
Gt.
mp
mf
mf
f
f
(chimes steady, non accel.)
f
f
Sw./Gt.
gradually to almost Full Organ
𝅗𝅥 = c. 60, but not ever synchronized with bells or left hand
Sw. to Ped.
rit.
più f
dim.
reduce slowly to Gt. alone; 8' Gemshorn + Fl. only
pp
(reduce to Fl. 16' + 8')
dim.
f
mf
mp
p
pp
pp
(Homage to C.E.I.)
6
poco rubato
Sw./Gt.
Sw. 8', warm stops
p
Gt.
10

Registrations by Marilyn Keiser.

Sept. 6, 1981 Ann Arbor

in memory of Marvin Gaye

10. Sometimes I Feel

WILLIAM BOLCOM
1984

10
sffz
simile
12
Trpts. or similar stops
f
add 16'
14
8' only
cresc.
cresc.
16
ff
add 16'
ff

8' only
add 16'
cresc.
cresc.
20
ff
cresc.
fff
ff
f
f
22
8' only
dim.
mf
mp
mf
p
mp
24
(non rit.)
4' 8' soft or 4' only
ancora dim.
più leggero

71

August 31, 1984 Ann Arbor

à la mémoire de Mme. Simone Plé-Caussade

11. Sweet Hour of Prayer

WILLIAM BOLCOM

Calmly; a comfortable tempo, not fast, in 8ths

*V = slight breath-marks

8
11
mp
mp
14
mf
mf
17
change registration;
whiter in sound
f, not
harsh
f

Sept. 8, 1984 Ann Arbor

12. Free Fantasia on "O Zion, Haste" and "How Firm a Foundation"

Full organ

WILLIAM BOLCOM

Copyright © 1987, 1994 by Edward B. Marks Music Company and Bolcom Music.
International Copyright Secured   All Rights Reserved

14
A little slower
dim.
pp
ppp
16' flute only
pp
ppp
6
Not too fast
mp
different manuals
With more movement
mf (sempre legato)
mp
mf (sempre legato)
(ppp)
accel.
Almost fast
less smooth
add 16', 4' f
cresc. poco a poco

add 4', 2'
accel. poco
ff
cresc. molto
Presto
fff
sub. ppp
Slow
n
8', 16'
p
pp
16' only
ppp
Gradually add stops
accel. poco a poco
7
cresc.
10
f
Poco maestoso, ma allegro - rubato
Full Organ

13
poco accel.
rall.
reduce to 8'
Free, rhapsodic (moderato)
sweet tone, like a clarinet
dim.
mp
sfz
p
change stops on beat
change stops on beat
16
quasi
rit.
p
p 8' Fl.
pp
16' only, soft stops
19
Moderato
Free
dim.
pp
mf, piercing, 8', 2'
sfz
fp
soft flutes and similar stops
pp
(pp)
21
rapide
accel.
pp
ppp

* $\cdot \circ \cdot = \circ$

** However, eighths remain equal or nearly so.

35
p
3
39
pp
p
8', 4'
Gt. bright sound
mp
add extra 16'
43
simile
simile
46

49
add more stops to Gt. + Ped.
mf
mp
mf
52
add more stops
cresc. poco a poco
55
(both manuals) as you can
58
more and more abandoned, but don't speed
+ Trpts.
simile
ff
Gt.
ff

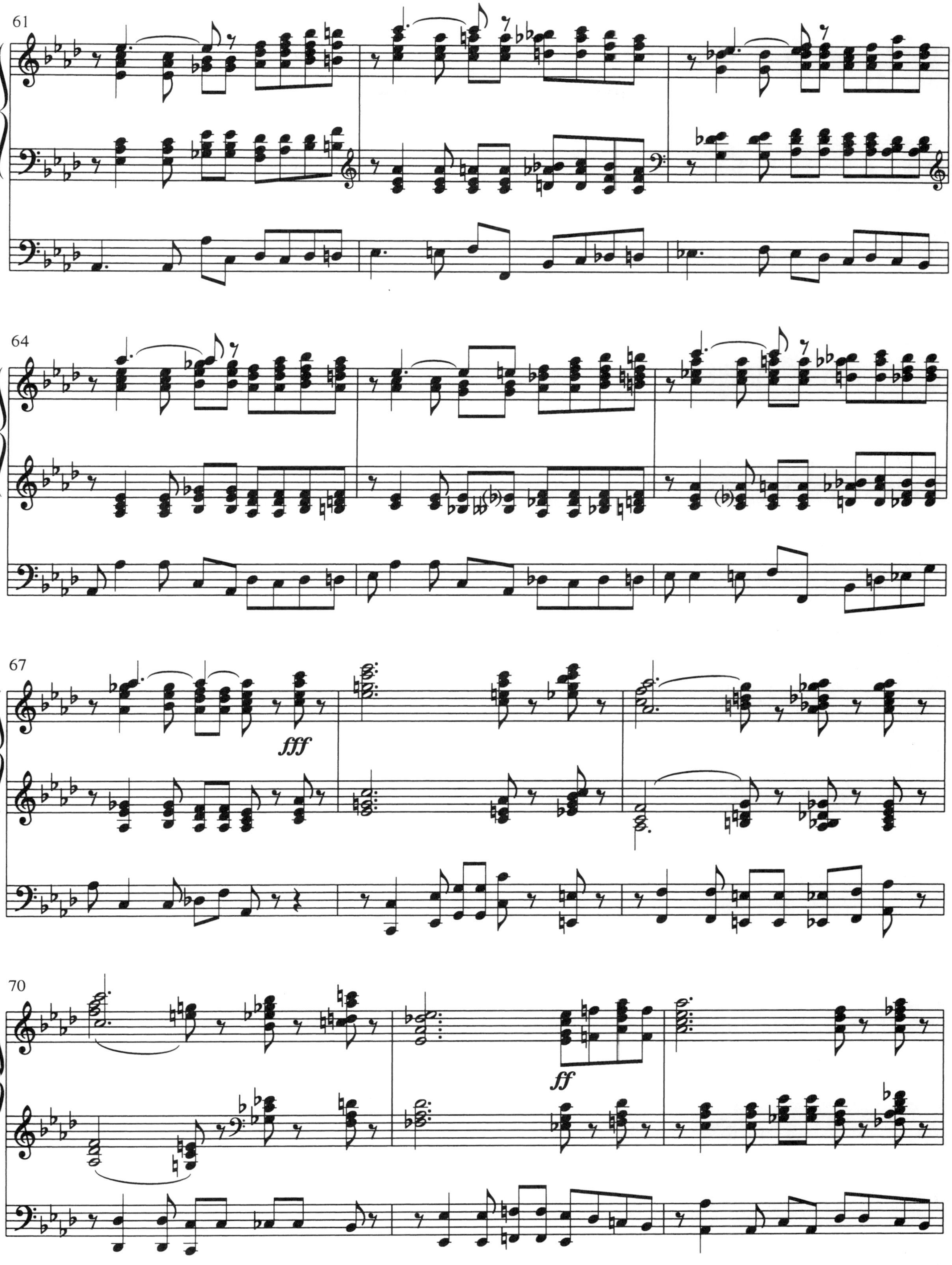
61
64
67
fff
70
ff

84

September 16, 1984 Ann Arbor

Chorale Prelude on "Abide with Me"

Choir (L.H. melody): Soft Oboe or soft Krumhorn
or mild Principal
Swell (Accompaniment): Soft Flutes and Strings
Pedal: to match accompaniment

WILLIAM BOLCOM
1970

in memory of Robert S. Bolcom
died October 15, 1970

Oct. 19, 1970

PROGRAM NOTES

BOOK 1 (1979)
What a Friend We Have in Jesus! is characterized by bold, jazzy harmonies, swinging rhythms and augmented melody. It has become one of the most popular and widely played settings among concert organists.
La Cathédrale engloutie (Rock of Ages) is directly related by title and opening motive to Claude Debussy's piano prelude, Book One, No. 10. It is one of the most abstract and atonal settings — based on fragments of the hymn tune, "Rock of Ages." The climax features a full organ, "mutated" hymn tune which uses two different keys simultaneously, similar in technique to the innovative American composer Charles Ives.
Just As I Am is a more straightforward, unornamented hymn tune setting constructed largely by the use of ostinatos and canons.

BOOK 2 (1980)
Jesus Loves Me is a tranquil setting of this children's song written in a conservative, contrapuntal Neo-Baroque style. Contributing to this style is the pervasive use of mordents.
Shall We Gather at the River is an animated and abstract setting which juxtaposes tonal hymn tune fragments against an atonal accompaniment. This setting imitates the flowing of the "river" through cascading keyboard patterns depicting various twists and rocks along its path.
Amazing Grace is the largest setting within this collection, written in Theme and Variations form. The five variations incorporate distinct and contrasting styles — from gospel, theater-organ, Baroque (quoting J. S. Bach's *Canonic Variations on "Von Himmel hoch"* BWV 769a) and jazz to atonal.

BOOK 3 (1981)
Jesus Call Us; O'er the Tumult is an intimate, slow setting with an unornamented hymn tune. It is written in a chromatic, four-voice texture and structured much like a typical Dietrich Buxtehude chorale prelude. There is a "mirror" relationship between the beginning and ending notes.
Blessed Assurance is one of the more purely exclamatory settings, indicated by the composer's marking "robust; like a shock!" This piece is set completely in chords, producing a massive, punctuated sound. It also uses ostinatos and stretto, where each half of the hymn tune is combined with the other and played simultaneously.
Nearer, My God, to Thee is a kind of "mutated," nebulous setting which includes a section to be played by optional handbells. There are passages in free meter as well as others that require playing in different time signatures simultaneously. This produces a very free, "non-synchronized" setting. The composer has included the inscription "Homage to C.E.I." (Charles Edward Ives) at this point in the score.

BOOK 4 (1984)
Sometimes I Feel was written in memory of the great Motown soul artist Marvin Gaye, who had been shot and killed by his own father just a few months earlier. It is written in a mostly jazz-chordal style with a swinging bass line played by the pedal.
Sweet Hour of Prayer is a gentle, polyphonic, highly chromatic setting — reminiscent of the style of Max Reger - with an unornamented melody.
Free Fantasia on "O Zion, Haste" and "How Firm a Foundation" is a combination of two smaller, contrasting settings, one following the other. "O Zion, Haste" is an atonal, through-composed, unmetered setting; whereas "How Firm a Foundation" is a tonal, strophic, metered (5/4) setting. "How Firm" is the finale to the whole collection, written in an uplifting and rousing gospel style.

Chorale Prelude on "Abide With Me" (1970) is an early prelude (not part of the *Gospel Preludes* set) written a few days after the death of Bolcom's father. It is a short, mournful setting treated in a four-voice Baroque style. Each phrase of the melody (played in the left hand) is separated by short interludes.

— Michael Mazzatenta